D0900307

ANT NOISES AT THE SAATCHI GALLERY

Jake and Dinos Chapman
Damien Hirst
Gary Hume
Sarah Lucas
Ron Mueck
Chris Ofili
Richard Patterson
Jenny Saville
Gavin Turk
Rachel Whiteread

Sponsored by

THE INDEPENDENT
ON SUNDAY

Jake and Dinos Chapman

By combining both their creative and destructive forces, the Chapmans make us question our own understanding of creativity. Is the point in the making, or what it is they make?

DNA Zygotic is a child who was lovingly built to suffer. It is a Siamese twin from feet to waist which mutates into a twelve-headed monstrous girl. This mannequin manipulation describes Chapman house of horror with less emphasis on the sexual body parts. Here the re-arrangement of pre-pubescent pussies is as unsettling as if they were extra ears or eyes in mis-matched places.

Unlike their earlier work, this does not quite seem seedy enough to be a sex toy. The only sexually unsettling aspect is that it is based on under-age girls. Perhaps the most frightening part of the sculpture is that it does not look distressed - there is no sign that a struggle has gone on.

The *Disasters of War* etchings give us an insight into the brain of the Chapmans and their fascination with Goya. Each small etching has been delicately hand painted with watercolour. The images are overwhelming in their intricacy of detail, describing mutilated bodies, disproportionate body parts and full-on scenes of explicit violence. Seen en masse they read like the preparations made by a crazed serial killer ready for action.

Damien Hirst

Damien Hirst has two styles: cold and clinical or bright and decorative. *Contemplating a Self-Portrait (as a Pharmacist)* is a reconstruction of the way a traditional artist would work - the only thing missing is the actual artist. Hirst's trademark vitrine contains an artist's smock and easel, with an unfinished painting and some tubes of paint dropped onto the floor. This is a romantic way to look at the image of the artist, but the construction suggests that access is not permitted. Hirst forces a common stereotype to be seen as a prison whilst suggesting that within the confinement there is some unfinished activity.

Hirst plays tricks on the viewer. *Horror at Home* is the perfect white minimal object - round and clean - but as you approach you see it is filled with the contents of hundreds of filthy ashtrays. He makes us believe that we are looking at something perfect that has been tarnished, but in doing so he takes the emphasis away from art and replaces it with an honest aspect of life.

A framed canvas in the shape of a love-heart, painted with sugar pink gloss paint and a sprinkling of glorious butterflies, bridges the gap between the sculpture and the paintings. Hirst uses butterflies as a metaphor for death. By having them settled on the surface of these gloss canvases they also read as a formal element; like the spots. Visually he gives us the very motif of love and romance. It is sweet, light and elegant, but close up it is an open grave.

Hymn is Damien Hirst's only sculpture literally to describe a human form. This anatomical description of the 'body' stands at a staggering 20 feet tall. The structure, made in bronze, is a sturdy and impenetrable version of fragile tissue and flesh, showing the internal organs that keep us alive. *Hymn* presents us with exposed life, the make-up and functions within its body, are revealed in bright colour. Although using a model of a human being has eliminated the metaphor, we are still held at a distance; this is the physical proof of how our life works but it shows us the only thing we will never see in ourselves. In *Hymn,* Hirst has built the object of his desire – a man who will live forever.

Gary Hume

Gary Hume's paintings seem to slow down time, forcing their presence gently onto us. The images are pieced together from separate sections of colour using high gloss household paint.

Referring to good things from recent times in art, Hume takes the graphic immediacy of Pop Art, the lyricism of abstract expressionism and the unadulterated beauty of decoration and rolls them into a single style. By using colours which are chic, domestic and fashionable, Gary Hume reminds us of the luxuries in life that are designed to make us feel good.

Hume's recent work has moved in a new direction. The "Water Painting" *3* is taken from a linear drawing of a beautiful girl, which is then overlaid as an image again and again. As you focus on the faces and features they seem to jump back and forth from different planes within the painting. Hume has found a way to add an illusion of depth to the image without using perspective. He re-creates a similar effect to that of staring at the surface of water, where your own image is distorted by light and surrounding reflections. Although we have always accepted the light within Hume's paintings as a formal element, he has now made the way we experience the image equally unpredictable and transitory. Hume makes a painting with a subject and surface that adheres to its place in time, but which forever after will always appear as fleeting.

Sarah Lucas

Sarah Lucas takes a literal expression and translates it into a physical object. She asserts her tough girl attitude by using cliché, puns and visual scenarios that would be more commonly found in the mind of a Ben Sherman shirt wearing lager boy.

Human Toilet is a photograph of the artist naked. Lucas poses as half woman, half toilet. By including herself in the image it stretches beyond being a surreal representation and becomes more like a joke at her own expense. *Down Below* combines a solid steel bathtub with a fluid seeping out from the plughole and onto the ground. Grubby and worn, it recalls a feeling of wanting to slip away. With no sign of disturbance or damage, it seems as if the daily activity of having a bath became the route for escape.

You Know What is a plaster cast of the artist from the waist down with a cigarette sticking out from between her legs. The casual pose is more defiant than sexy suggesting, "If I haven't got a mouth I'll smoke out my pussy".

By contrast, in *Self Portrait with Cigarettes* Lucas opts for the softer side of a boy's fantasy; a gentle girl made out of cigarettes, waiting to be smoked away. This work introduces a shift. Lucas is no longer the angry young woman with a score to settle. She draws a thoughtful self-portrait showing herself as wide-eyed and passive. Sarah Lucas is working with similar materials to those she has always used, but her ideas are now presented without the gender and identity angst.

Ron Mueck

Looking at a Ron Mueck sculpture is like looking at the world according to an emotional reaction.

The attention to detail and the variations in scale make the sculptures feel as if they belong to their own world, where how you feel is reflected in how you look. In *Mask* Mueck describes anger as a physicality by literally blowing his face up. His own scowling face is enlarged to over 5 feet tall. *Big Baby* reminds us that giving immeasurable joy makes you become a beautiful enlargement of yourself in everyone's eyes. *Angel* is a sculpture of a small man seated on a stool. He is not one of Giotto's cherubs - he is more like the angel from next door. He has a pair of wings that identify him as a non-human creature but he is not the kind of angel we have been led to believe in. Clearly not an angel of Italian churches he is just as fragile and vulnerable. Middle aged and slightly awkward, sad looking and down trodden, Mueck's angel clarifies what we perceive as divine. Through responding to this angel's vulnerability and sadness, we experience something as beautiful as what we see in traditional angels.

Chris Ofili

Chris Ofili uses collage cut-outs from porn magazines, masses of beads of paint, pours of resin, and touches of glitter which he spreads out on the canvas creating the shapes and forms of comic-book-style fictive characters or energising abstract patterns. His issues of identity are disguised within the activity of making a highly decorative abstract or figurative painting. The awkwardness of the subject matter is released into the process and not forced onto the viewer.

Richard Patterson

Richard Patterson acts out the ultimate painting fantasy by placing figuration and abstraction together to exist on equal terms.

In *Culture Station - Zipper*, the central focus is a strip of pure and perfect figuration. It lies sandwiched between five stark panels that build up a hard abstract container. Patterson forces the two styles to sit beside each other without distorting or favouring either. His piecing together of panels explores the structure of composition within a painting, rather than just within an image. The subject we see is playful hedonism; the designer life aboard the luxury yacht with a gleaming motorbike surrounded by a group of beautiful people. In choosing a glamorous BSA advert as his image, Patterson makes the subject as seductive for the viewer as the process of painting is for him.

Patterson is using a style and an image which both represent an idea of perfection. By incorporating a pictorial illusion of pleasure into an abstract painting he slots life and light into what would otherwise be cold, formal abstraction.

Jenny Saville

Jenny Saville makes large paintings of large women. She uses scale as a device to engulf the viewer and creates intimacy by shrinking us down. Saville's paintings are filled with subtle tonal shifts in colour which pull us into a world of flesh.

In *Fulcrum* Saville uses the geometry of the canvas physically to push the bodies into every edge, making the image claustrophobic and uncomfortable. Close up the bodies appear as abstract coloured slabs of flesh packed and squeezed like raw meat. The primary aim of this painting is to get the paint to resemble types of skin and flesh as closely as possible. She wants us to be uncertain whether we are looking at the way paint behaves when describing the body, or the way the body looks when it is described with paint.

Saville's paintings have evolved. They are less angry and less dominated by their politics. She has dropped using "fat as a feminist issue" and become fully engrossed with the actual process of painting a large body. She describes with confidence her own fascination with the physicality of women's bodies and how they behave.

Gavin Turk

Gavin Turk is a master of disguise. His obsession with being a celebrity has become a skill for making work that explores the myth of the artist. He has built his own identikit image of himself as a celebrity by adopting the status attached to other celebrities. Gavin Turk explores the cult of glamour within the Art world using imagery from the world at large.

When Turk goes undercover the viewer is forced to re-evaluate the idea of originality in art, and the experience of seeing art. In *Che Gavara* not only are we given an altered version of a well-known historical image but we also see Turk inventing himself as an icon of rebellion. He makes us question whether the celebrity status that attracts us is more important than the work that has been made by creating friction between style and content. *Pimp* is out of synch with the usual look of Turk's sculpture, but actually covers similar territory. Although *Pimp* is essentially an industrial skip, it is not strictly a ready-made as it has been manufactured to order. Turk presents the skip as though it is a found object, and uses it to make a pastiche of minimalist sculpture. Instead of making himself the star through art, he lets the criteria for judging an established art-concept promote an ordinary object.

Turk uses the connotations of the object to mock the clean, polished monumental style of minimalist abstraction. Caught idle, between form and function, *Pimp* is empty - just like star status.

Rachel Whiteread

Untitled, (One Hundred Spaces) are the unseen areas which occupy the underneath of one hundred chairs. These brightly coloured semi-transparent resin cubes read as formalist colour blocks that activate the space they are in. They span the entirety of the gallery like lined up soldiers, each one placed a particular distance from the next. These coloured cubes make emptiness become a physical reality and the surrounding space is subverted by their existence. What has now become the negative space remains empty.

Instead of waiting for remains of previous lives to be discovered, Rachel Whiteread has developed her own means of archaeology. By casting these non-existent spaces from beneath one hundred different chairs Whiteread indirectly refers to human presence and reminds us of the intimate sense of belonging signified by a chair. She makes an emotionally charged installation from a basic object that is easily overlooked.

By making something which has zero status exist, Whiteread has altered the identity of the original object. Suddenly the function of the original seems irrelevant and vacant. Within this group of casts there is no recognisable or definable characteristic except the relationships between the forms and the spaces they are in.

GEMMA DE CRUZ

Jake and Dinos Chapman *D.N.A. Zygotic* 1997 fibreglass, resin and paint 190 x 90 x 90cm / 74¾ x 35½ x 35½in

NIKE
NIKE
NIKE
NIKE

Jake and Dinos Chapman *Disasters of War* 2000 83 hand-coloured etchings 24.5 x 34.5cm / 9⅝ x 13⅝in

BAD
FUCK IT
TESTICLE MITE

EXCREMENT

Damien Hirst *Horror at Home* 1995 GRP composites, foam and contents of ashtray height 70cm / 27½in; diameter 244cm / 96in

Damien Hirst *Contemplating a Self Portrait (as a Pharmacist)* 1998 steel, glass and contents 213.4 x 304.8 x 274.3cm / 84 x 120 x 108in

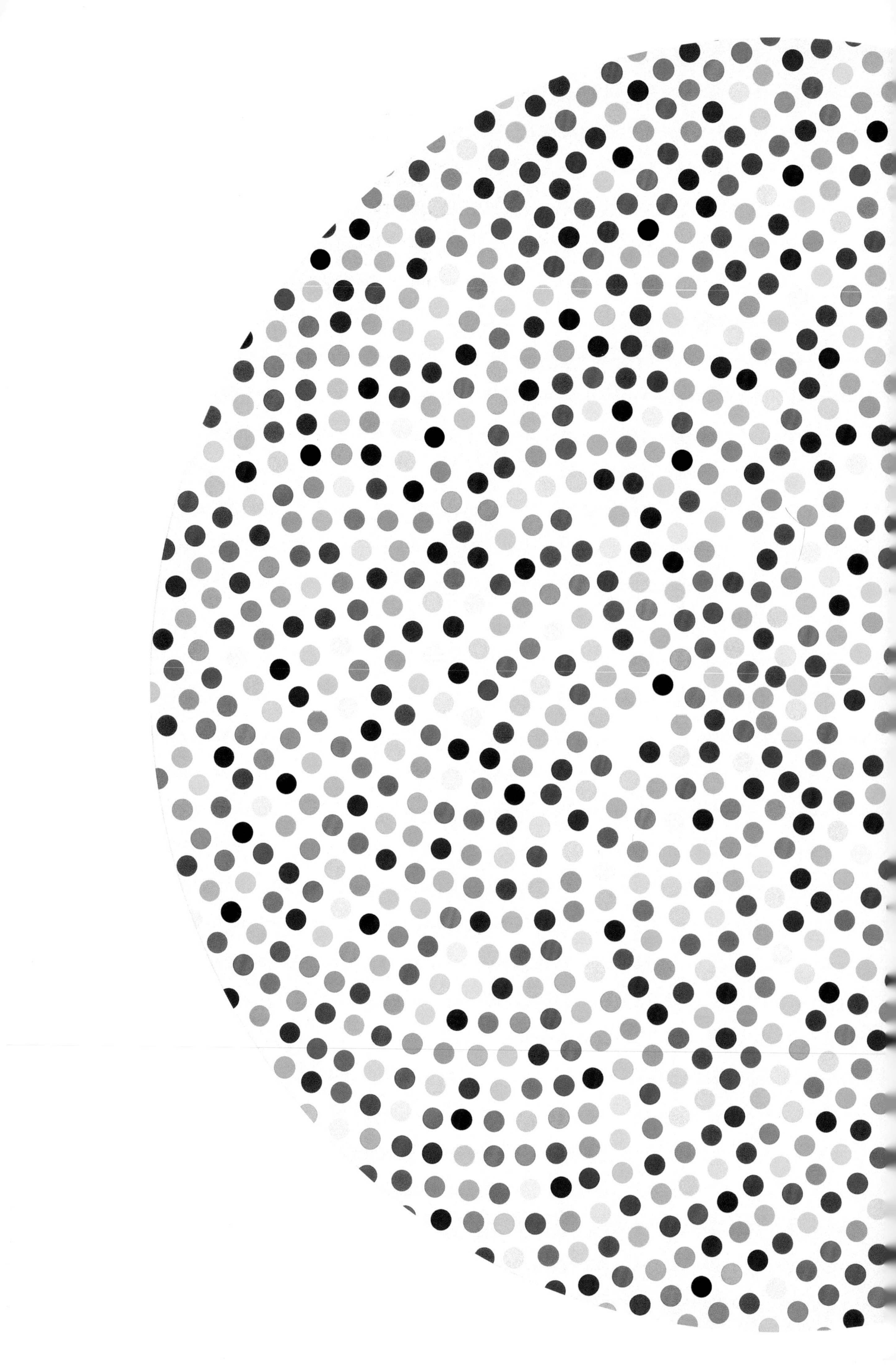

Damien Hirst *Zeolite Mixture* 1999 gloss household paint on canvas 304.8cm / 120in diameter

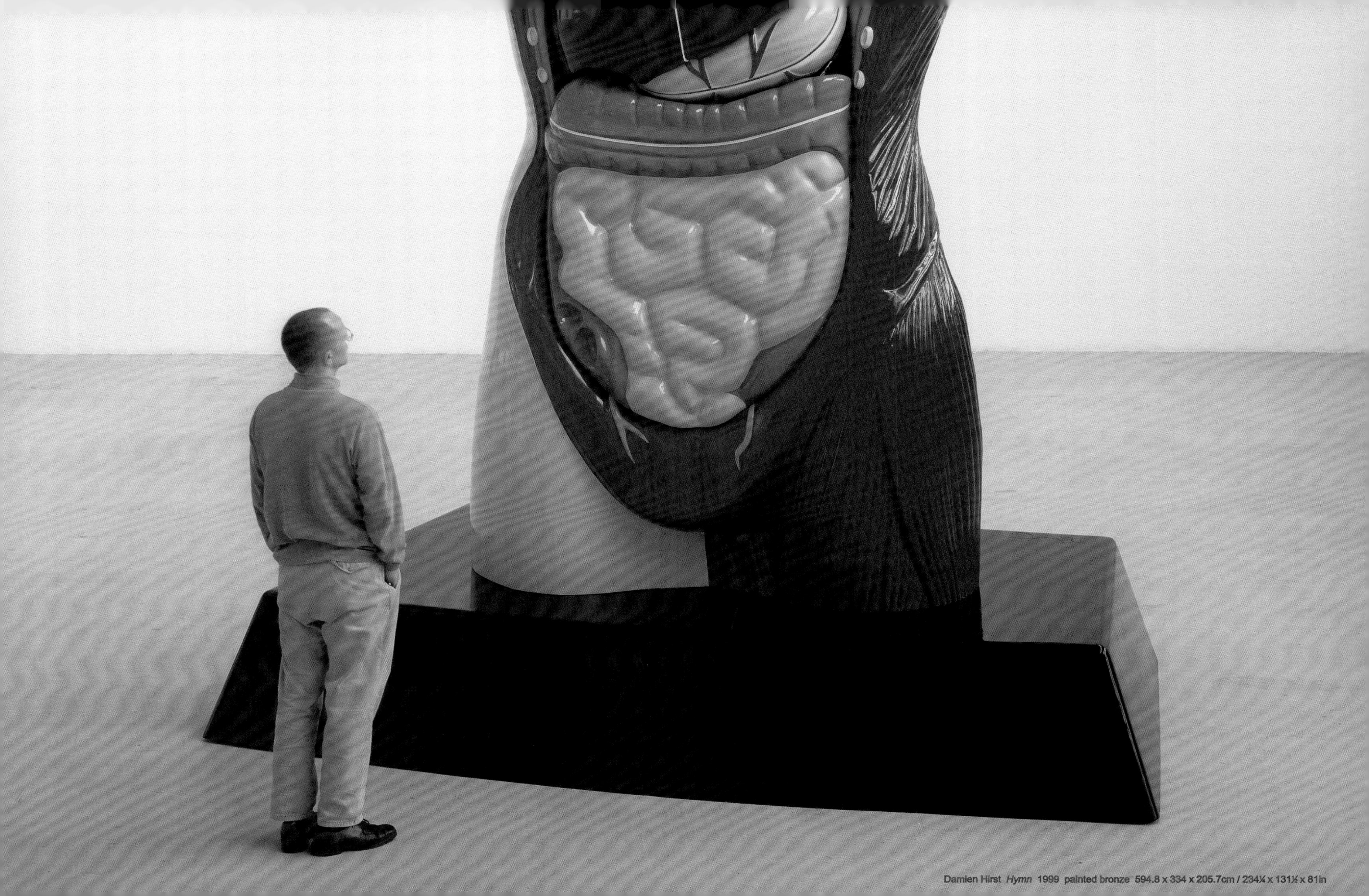

Damien Hirst *Hymn* 1999 painted bronze 594.8 x 334 x 205.7cm / 234¼ x 131½ x 81in

Gary Hume *Like Father Like Son* 1998 household paint on aluminium and mixed media 200 x 162cm / 78¾ x 63¾in

Gary Hume *Bird Point III* 1998 gloss paint on aluminium 221 x 492cm / 87 x 194in

Gary Hume *3* 2000 enamel paint on aluminium panel 305 x 241.3cm / 120 x 95in

Sarah Lucas *Human Toilet* 1997 colour print 244 x 188.5cm / 96 x 74in

Sarah Lucas *Down Below* 1997 enamel bath, rubber, acrylic 55 x 60.5 x 165cm / 21¾ x 23¾ x 65in spill: 193 x 179cm / 76 x 70½in

Sarah Lucas *Self Portrait With Cigarettes* 2000 brown paper, cigarettes 266 x 180cm / 104¾ x 71in

Sarah Lucas *You Know What* 1998 plaster, cigarette, table 85.1 x 78.7 x 94cm / 33½ x 31 x 37in

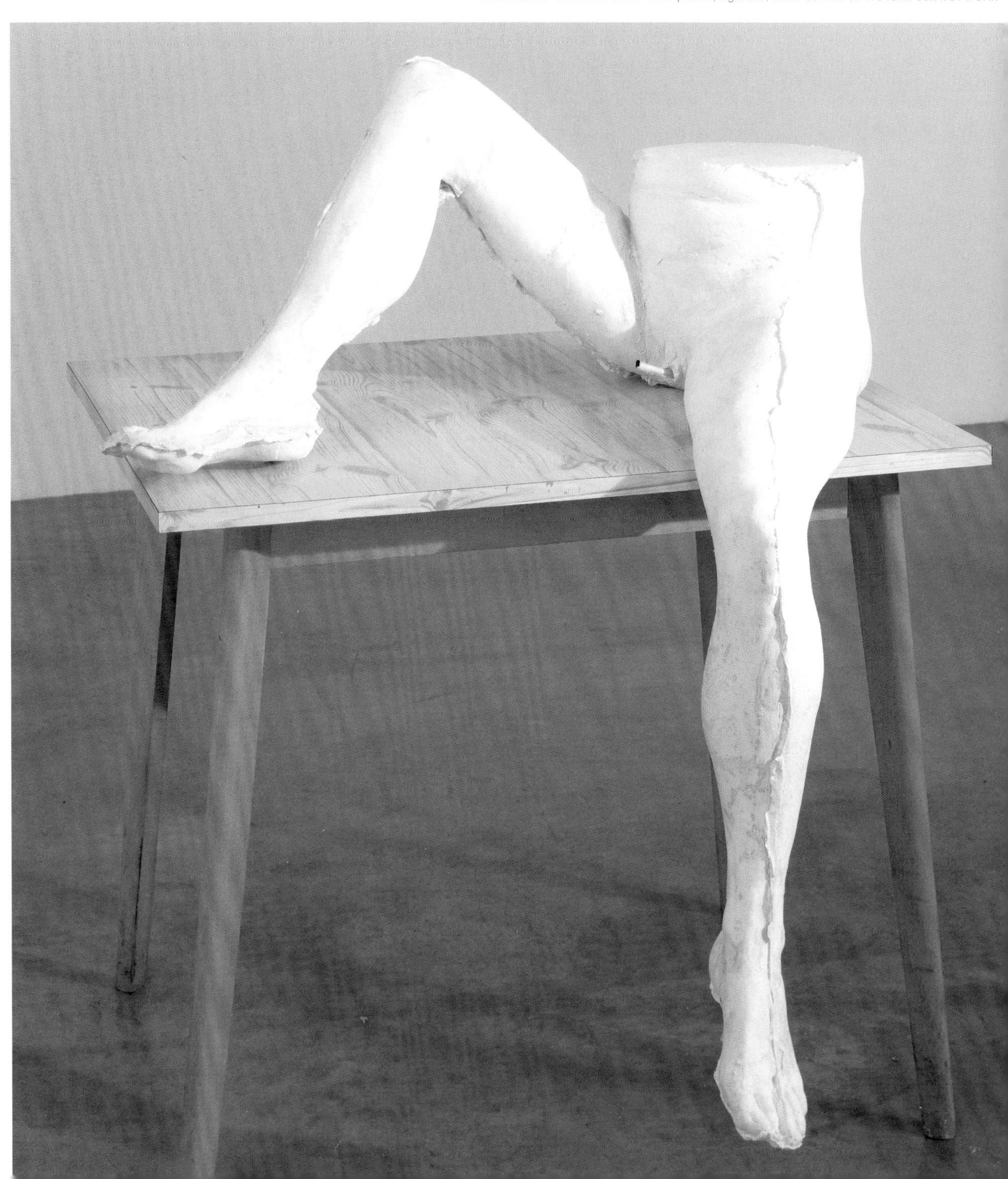

Sarah Lucas *Dreams Go Up In Smoke* 2000 cast bronze and cigarettes 142 x 82 x 62cm / 60 x 32¼ x 24½in

Ron Mueck *Mask* 1997 polyester resin and mixed media 158 x 153 x 124cm / 62¼ x 60¼ x 48¾in

Ron Mueck *Angel* 1997 silicone rubber and mixed media 110 x 87 x 81cm / 43¼ x 34¼ x 32in

Ron Mueck *Pinocchio* 1996 polyester resin, fibreglass and human hair 84 x 20 x 18cm / 33 x 8 x 7in

Ron Mueck *Big Baby* 1996; *Big Baby 3* 1996-7 mixed media 85 x 71 x 70cm / 33½ x 28 x 27½in; 86 x 81 x 70 / 34 x 32 x 27½in

Chris Ofili *Four Plus One More* 1998 mixed media on canvas 182.9 x 121.9cm / 72 x 48in

Chris Ofili *Untitled* 1998 mixed media on canvas 190.5 x 120cm / 75 x 47¼in

Chris Ofili *x + y = 0* 2000 mixed media on canvas 243.8 x 365.8cm / 96 x 144in

Richard Patterson *Culture Station - Zipper* 1995 oil and acrylic on canvas 213.4 x 459.7cm / 84 x 181in

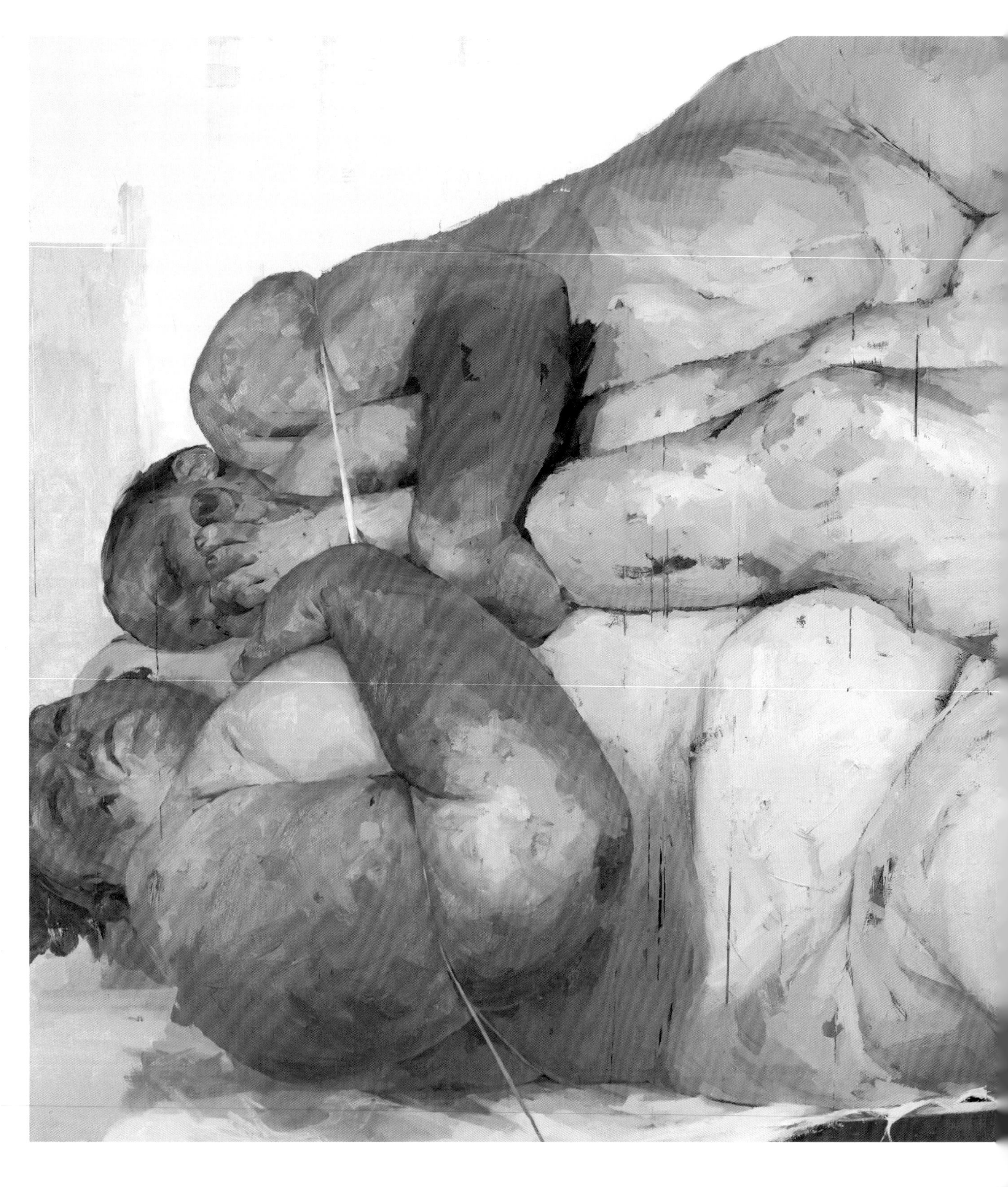

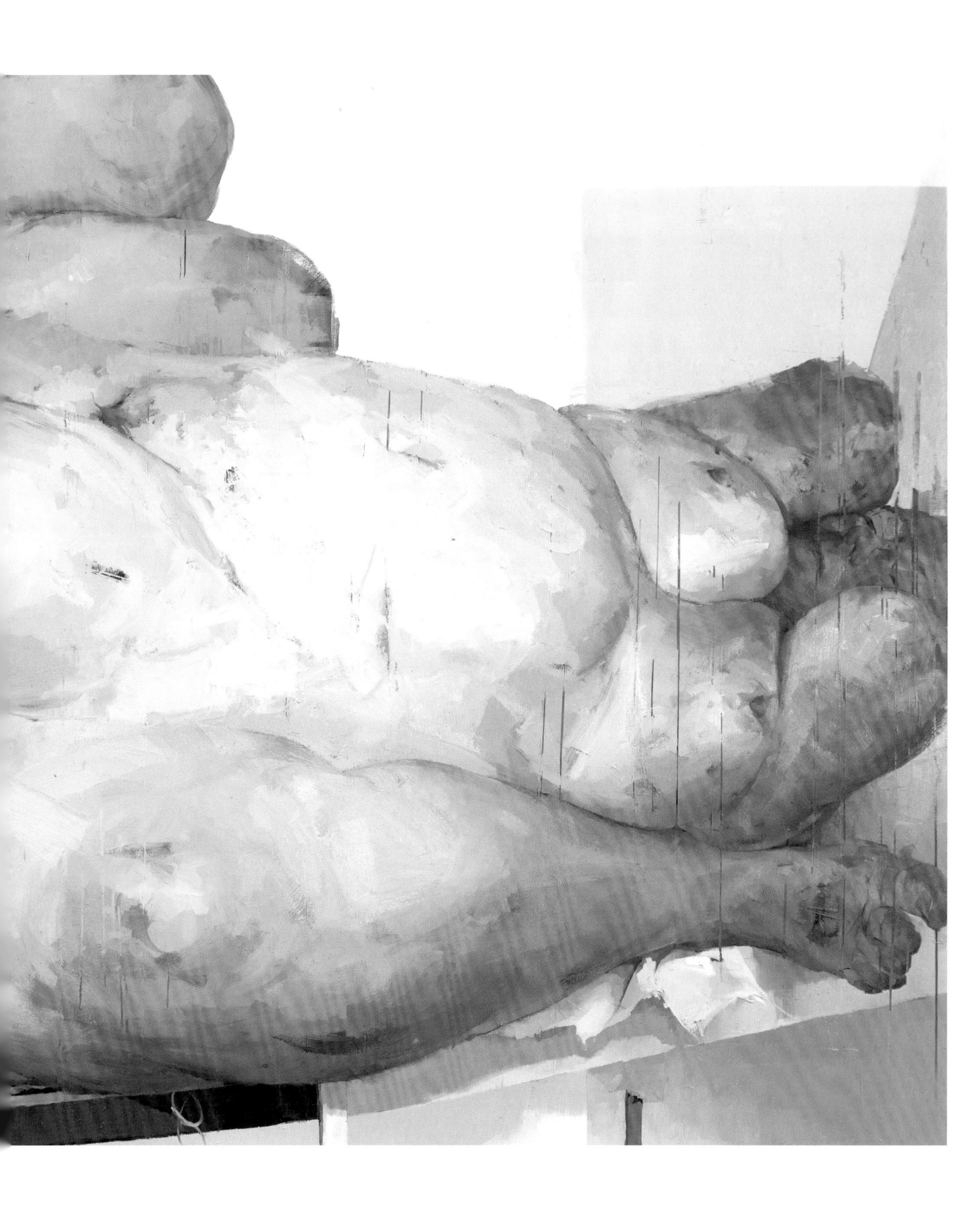

Jenny Saville *Fulcrum* 1999 oil on canvas 261.6 x 487.7cm / 103 x 193in

Jenny Saville *Hyphen* 1999 oil on canvas 274.3 x 365.8cm / 108 x 144in

Gavin Turk *Pimp* 1996 painted steel 183.5 x 373 x 184cm / 72¼ x 147 x 72½in

Gavin Turk *Oi!* 1998 three R-type photographs 244 x 609cm / 96¼ x 240in

Rachel Whiteread *Untitled (One Hundred Spaces)* 1995 resin 100 units, size according to installation

Gavin Turk *Che Gavara* 1999 billboard poster 304.8 x 792.5cm / 120 x 312in Originally commissioned by Channel Four for 'This is Modern Art' 1999